TINY TRAVELERS
FIND YOUR FOREST

Copyright © 2023 Encantos Media Studios, PBC.
TINY TRAVELERS™ and ENCANTOS®
are trademarks of Encantos Media Studios, PBC.
All rights reserved.

Library of Congress
Cataloging-in-Publication Data is available.
First edition, April 2023
Printed in China
ISBN 978-1-954689-29-9

Did you know that there are 574 Native American Tribes in the United States? Each of these Tribes has a unique connection to the land and different cultural practices. Please visit the Resources page at the end of the book to learn more.

May this book help you discover the adventures that await in your forest. —The Encantos Team

About the Authors
Audrey Noguera is a first-time author who takes long walks in the woods whenever possible.
She can be found wandering the forests of New Jersey with her dad and co-author Taylor Margis-Noguera.

About the Illustrator
Abigail Gross is a children's book illustrator based in Pennsylvania. A graduate of the Pratt Institute,
she has illustrated over fifteen books, most recently Kiki Can! Go to School.

About Tiny Travelers
Tiny Travelers was created by Steven Wolfe Pereira & Nuria Santamaria Wolfe to help kids become
"citizens of the world". Tiny Travelers brings to life culture, geography, history, and more so kids
can learn about the rich diversity of people and places around the globe.
tinytravelers.com

This book was created in collaboration with author Annie Margis, designed by Angie Monroy,
and edited by Susie Jaramillo, Jill Freshney, Carolina Dammert, and Olivia Conley.
Special thanks to Steven Wolfe Pereira and Dhatri Navanayagam,
as well as the teams at Target & Essence.

The text was set in Cooper and Prater Sans and the illustrations for this book
were created digitally.

Thank you to the Forest Service (an agency of the U.S. Department of Agriculture)
and the Ad Council, for providing input on this book. USDA is an equal opportunity
employer, provider, and lender.

For more information and to discover a park or forest near you, visit

DISCOVERtheFOREST.org

ad COUNCIL

TINY TRAVELERS
FIND YOUR FOREST

Encantos

Illustrated by Abigail Gross

Written by Audrey Noguera & Taylor Margis-Noguera

Sunscreen. Water bottle. Journal and snacks.
We have them all in our backpacks.
It's time to visit a forest.
The trees are waiting for us.

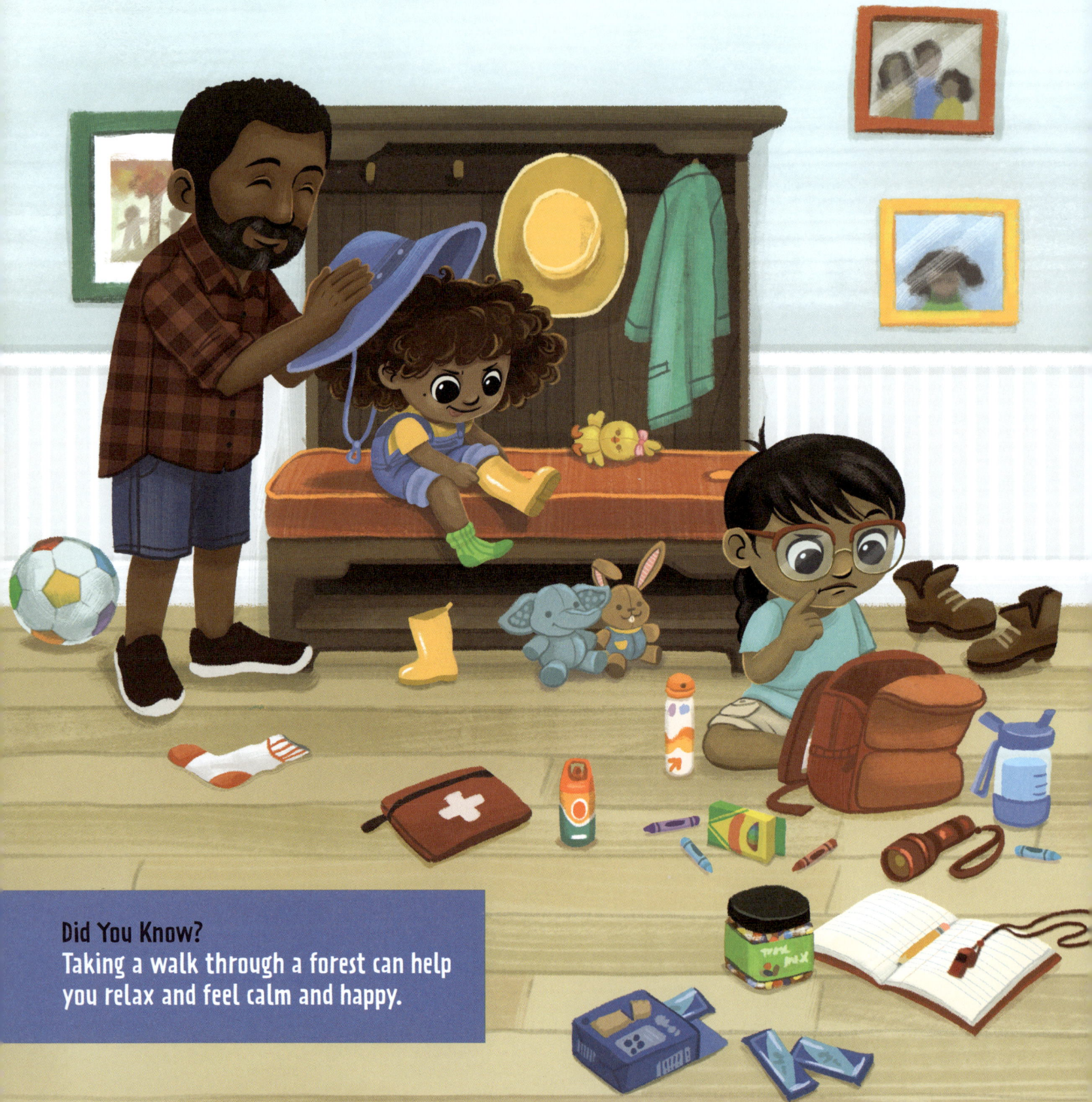

Did You Know?
Taking a walk through a forest can help
you relax and feel calm and happy.

But *how* do we find one?
On your feet, let's go explore
the forest right outside your door!

Packing List

- ☑ Sunscreen
- ☑ Water Bottle
- ☑ Snacks
- ☑ Binoculars
- ☑ Bug Spray
- ☑ Journal
- ☑ Hat
- ☑ Backpack
- ☑ Whistle

Trees in gardens. Trees on the street.
Trees in the park and on sidewalks concrete.
All the trees in your neighborhood
are an urban forest of leaves and wood.

Sycamore

Did You Know?
An arborist is a person whose job
is to plant and care for trees.
Fun job, right?

Arborist

Urban forests quiet city noise and cool the air.
They create shade here and there
and breathe out oxygen everywhere.

Trees make up a forest. But what makes up a tree?
A trunk with roots and branches with leaves.

Pin Oak

Dogwood

Some trees are tall,
and some trees are small,
and some are right in between.

Blue Jay

American
Hazelnut

Did You Know?
You can tell the age of a tree by counting its
rings. Each circle represents one year of growth.

Skin covers us like bark covers trees.
We're similar, except trees never skin their knees.

Red Maple

THE CROWN

Leaves & Branches

THE TRUNK

Bark

THE ROOTS

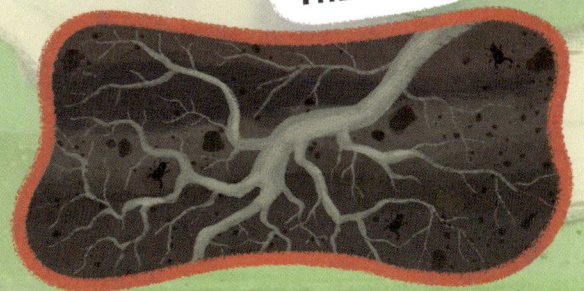

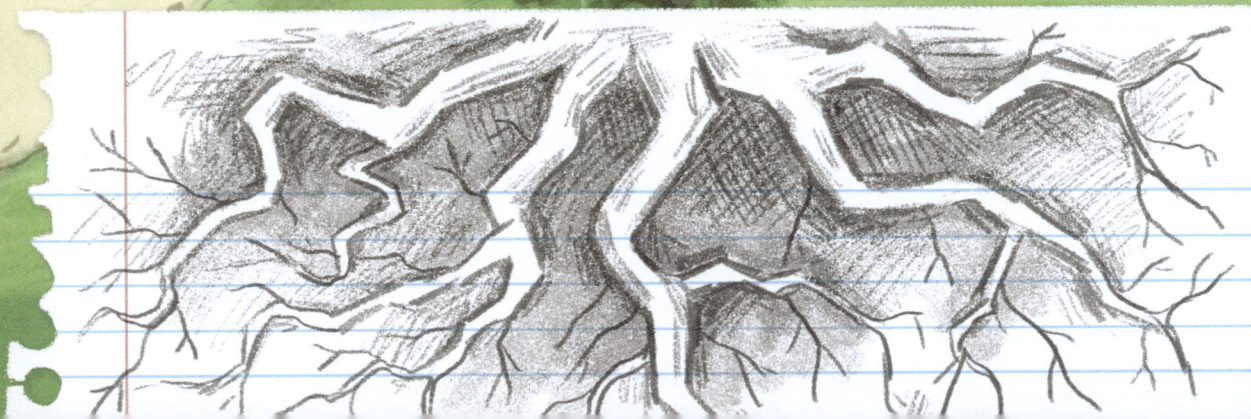

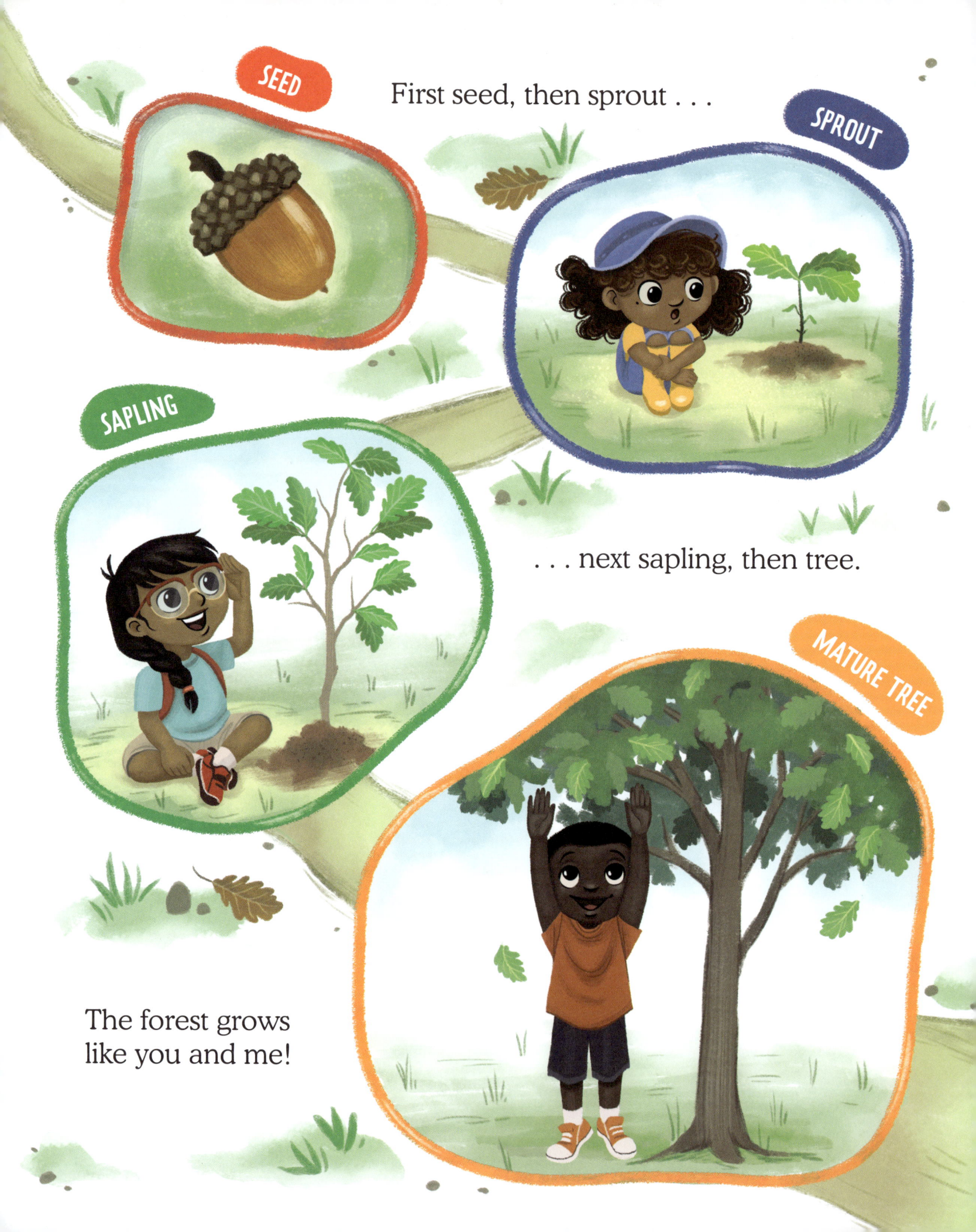

SEED

First seed, then sprout . . .

SPROUT

SAPLING

. . . next sapling, then tree.

MATURE TREE

The forest grows
like you and me!

A snag *(funny name!)* is a dead tree and home for the forest community.

SNAG

Red-Winged Blackbird

Eastern Screech Owl

Cottontail Rabbit

Turkey Tail Mushrooms

Did You Know?
Trees can live to be over a hundred years old; some live thousands of years!

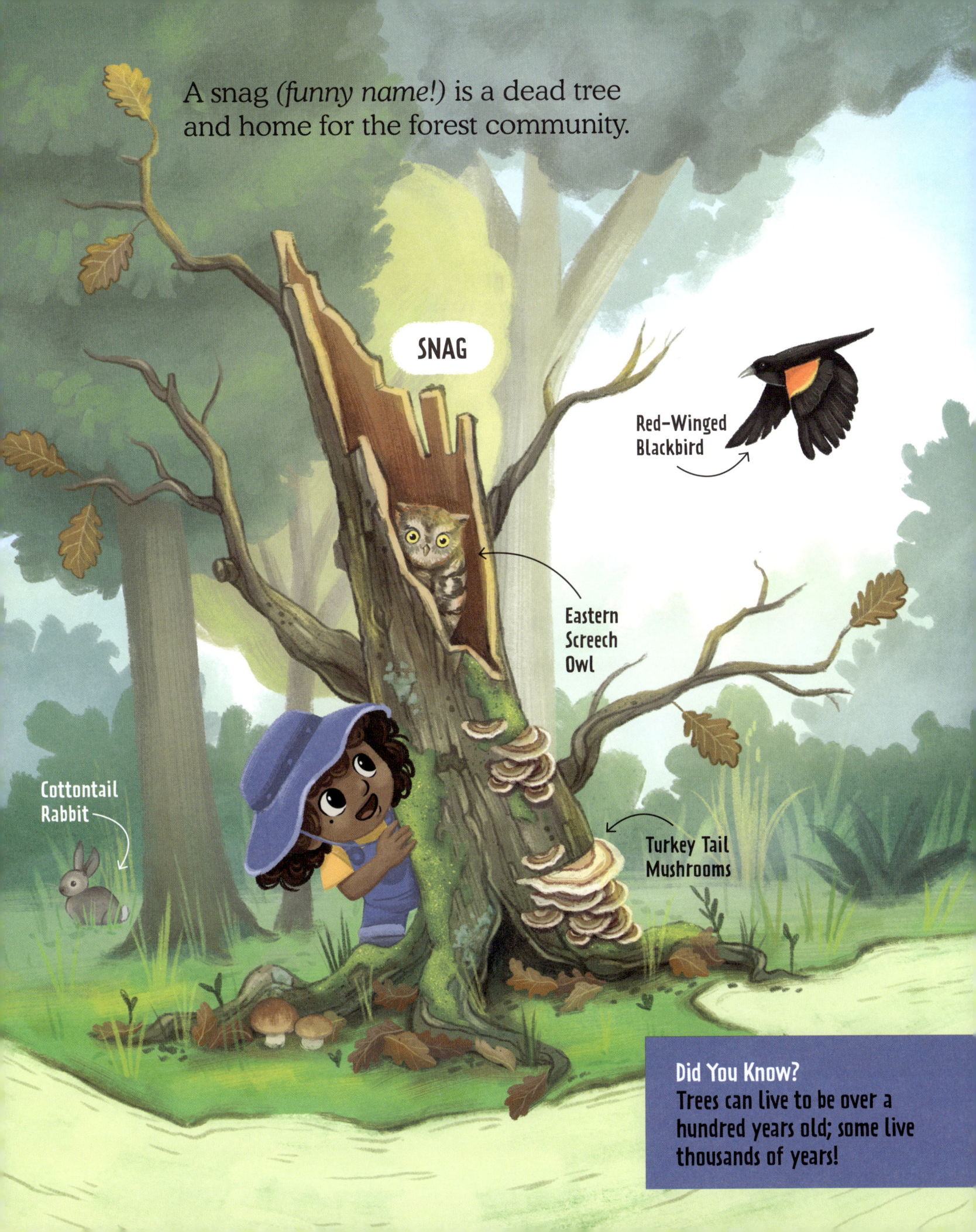

Let's go for a hike! Stay on trails along the way.

Catch falling leaves and listen as the trees sway, sway, sway.

How many creatures do you see?
Two? Or Three?
Look around at fungi too.
Lots of forest things to do.

Look, don't touch, is our advice
to keep our forests looking nice.

Red-Tailed Hawk

Quaking Aspen

Stay on Trail

Opossum

Sweet Gum

Red Fox

Coral Honeysuckle

Bolete Mushrooms

Did You Know?
Mushrooms are a common form of fungi.
They don't require sunlight to grow,
and some even glow in the dark!

Animal, plant, and insect kingdom
all play their part in the ecosystem.

Worms eat leaves, and frogs eat worms.
Herons eat frogs, and the cycle turns.

Peregrine Falcon

Great Blue Heron

Canada Goose

Mallard Duck

Eastern Box Turtle

Azaleas

Green Frog

Did You Know?
Frogs are carnivores, which means they will eat insects, worms, small mammals, fish, and even other frogs!

Black-Eyed Susans

Photosynthesis

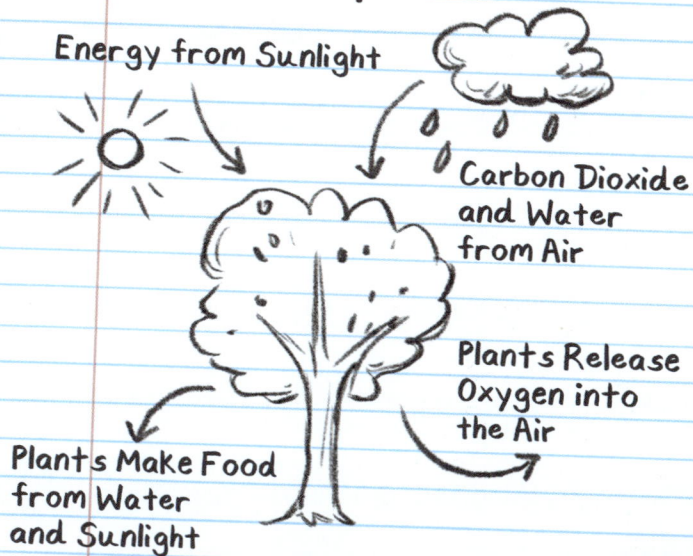

Energy from Sunlight

Carbon Dioxide and Water from Air

Plants Release Oxygen into the Air

Plants Make Food from Water and Sunlight

Weeping Willow

Cat Tails

Wood Ducks

Common Milkweed

Forests produce oxygen, which we can't live without,
filter drinking water, and help prevent a drought.

Trees turn sunlight into energy.
They are really good at chemistry.

Tropical forests are hot. Boreal forests are cold.

TROPICAL

BOREAL

Temperate forests are in between,
and most redwood forests are old.

TEMPERATE

REDWOOD

In winter, the leaves on some trees disappear.
In evergreen forests, you see leaves all year.

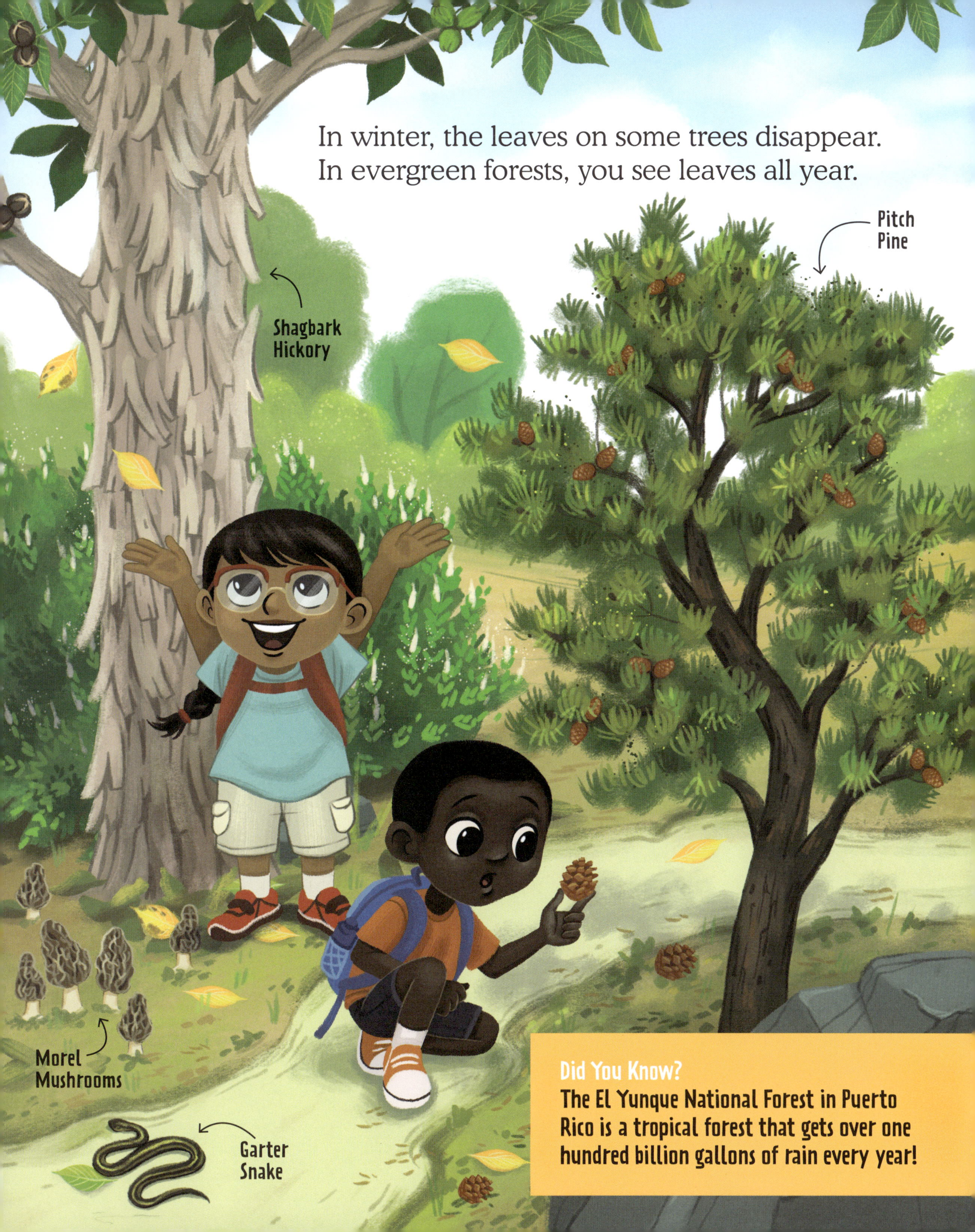

Pitch Pine
Shagbark Hickory
Morel Mushrooms
Garter Snake

Did You Know?
The El Yunque National Forest in Puerto Rico is a tropical forest that gets over one hundred billion gallons of rain every year!

Fauna and flora are animals and plants.
From moss on rocks to squirrels and ants.

Raccoon

Black
Walnut

White-Tailed Deer

Skunk
Cabbage

Chicken of the
Woods Mushrooms

Coneflowers

Eastern Gray Squirrel

Did You Know?
Trees communicate to each other through
their roots and through fungi to warn
about droughts, disease, and insect attacks!

Everything relies on the forest to survive.

FIREFLY

CHIPMUNK

The flashy, the furry,
the slimy, the tiny.
The feathered, the scaly,
the thorny, the viney.

SPOTTED SALAMANDER

LADYBUG

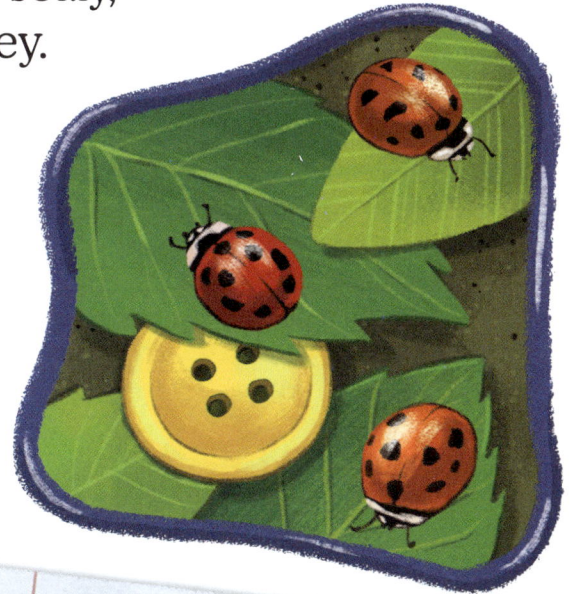

Even the shiny
help the forest thrive.

POISON IVY

Beware!

Poison ivy can make
you itchy if you touch it.

Just remember:
leaves of three, let them be.

Birds build nests from low to high.
They sing songs and happily fly
all across the countryside
gathering twigs from far and wide.

Northern
Flicker

American
Kestrel

Northern
Cardinal

Mourning
Dove

Black-Capped
Chickadee

Tufted
Titmouse

Song
Sparrow

Did You Know?
Ever wonder how birds can fly?
In addition to feathers, birds have hollow
bones that make them light for flight.

Ruby-Throated Hummingbird

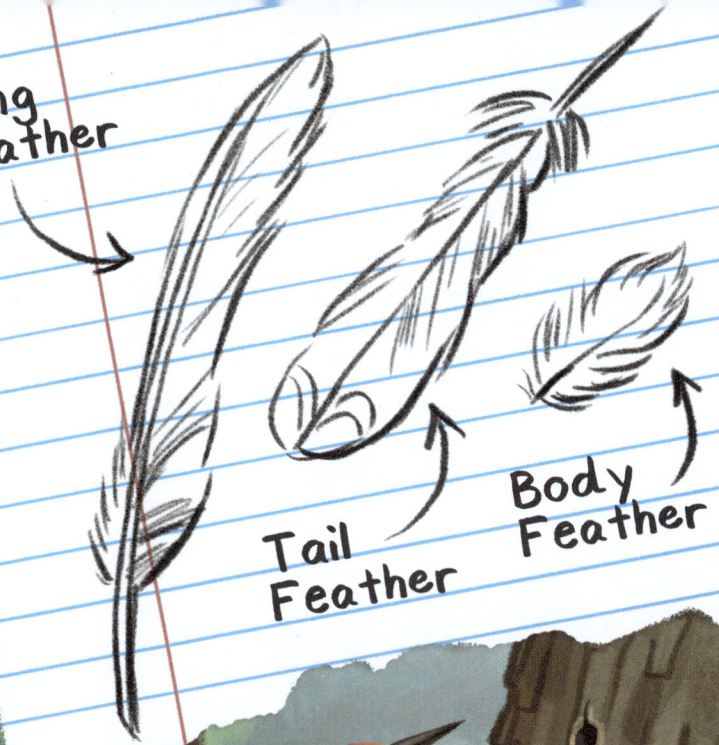
Wing Feather

Tail Feather

Body Feather

American Robin

Red-Bellied Woodpecker

Close your eyes and listen.
Can you hear a bird?
Open your eyes and look for it.
Find the bird you heard!

Northern Mockingbird

American Goldfinch

American Crow

Honey Bee

Earthworm

Forest beetles eat rotting wood,
and snails eat leaves of green.
Ants and spiders do their part
to keep the forest clean.

Bark
Centipede

Garden
Snail

Black
Ant

Mantis

Garden Spider

Bumblebee

Cecropia Moth

Cricket

Ground Beetle

Monarch Butterfly

Bees are good at pollination.
They help to make more flowers.
Some butterflies make long migrations,
flying for hours and hours.

Stag Beetle

Most of us, whether we know it or not,
use lots of forest goods.

LUMBER

FRUITS

BOOKS

American
Chestnut

Sustainable forestry means that we try
to give back as much as we take from the forest.

Look for these logos
when you are shopping
with your family.

SUSTAINABLE
FORESTRY
INITIATIVE

FSC®

PEFC™

Toilet paper, furniture, and even clothes are often made of wood!

TOILET PAPER

FURNITURE

CLOTHING

Did You Know?
Many Native American Tribes have used different types of forest plants as medicine for a very long time. The leaves of the American chestnut tree have been used as a remedy for colds. Chestnut seeds are a tasty food, and the wood can be used to build homes and furniture!

The forest is wild yet serene.
Let's always keep it safe and clean.

American
Elm

As you take
a look around,
leave the woods
as they were found.

Be respectful in this place.
Forests need their breathing space.

Eastern
White Pine

Activities

Leaf Rubbing

Let's create a leaf's twin on paper!
All you need is <u>a leaf</u>, <u>some paper</u>,
and your favorite <u>crayon</u>.

1. Find a leaf on the ground.
2. Put the leaf on a flat surface,
   and place a piece of blank paper
   on top of your leaf.
3. Rub your crayon over the paper.
4. The leaf appears! Isn't that amazing?
   Try it with different leaves and colors.

Sound Map

Let's make a map of forest sounds!
All you need is <u>a journal</u>, <u>your ears</u>,
and <u>something to write with</u>.

1. In your journal, put an X in the
   middle of a blank page. That's you.
2. Close your eyes and listen. What's
   making the sound you hear?
   Birds, bugs, the wind?
3. Open your eyes and mark where
   you heard each sound around you
   and what you think it is.

Look, you made a sound map!

Nature Journaling

Let's write about your forest adventure!

*All you need is **a journal** and **something to write with**.*

1. Write down all the things you did and heard and saw.

2. Draw pictures of the plants and animals and everything else you liked about the forest.

3. Make up a story about the forest.

Wow, you are a nature writer!

Northern Cardinal
* around 9 inches
* bright red (males)
* High-Pitched "Chip" sounds
* I saw 3 cardinals

Scavenger Hunt

Let's go on a scavenger hunt!

1. Bring an adult to help you look for these awesome forest finds!

Look in the book:
- ◯ Sycamore Tree
- ◯ Blue Jay
- ◯ Turkey Tail Mushroom
- ◯ Cottontail Rabbit
- ◯ Green Frog
- ◯ Earthworm

Look in the forest:
- ◯ A bird
- ◯ An insect
- ◯ A flower
- ◯ A rock
- ◯ A twig

BIRD

Resources

Family Nature Activities

* Science inquiry and career exploration resources: *naturalinquirer.org*

* Woodsy Owl and Smokey Bear educational resources: *apps.fs.usda.gov/symbols*

* Family nature activities: *plt.org/activities-for-families*

  fishwildlife.org/projectwild/wild-parents

* Supplies for environmental and nature education activities: *acornnaturalists.com*

Finding Outdoor Places to Explore

* Discover a park or forest near you: *discovertheforest.org*

* Trip planning for visiting public lands: *recreation.gov*

Learn More About Native American Tribes

* Taking a trip to Washington, DC, or New York, NY?

  Visit the National Museum of the American Indian and learn more about the rich history and culture of Native American Tribes. *americanindian.si.edu*

Find Your Forest Book Resources

Packing List

Backpack

Bug Spray

Flashlight

Sunscreen

SPF 50

Water Bottle

Whistle

Snacks

First Aid Kit

Packing List

Journal

Writing Tools

Comfortable Shoes

Sun Hat

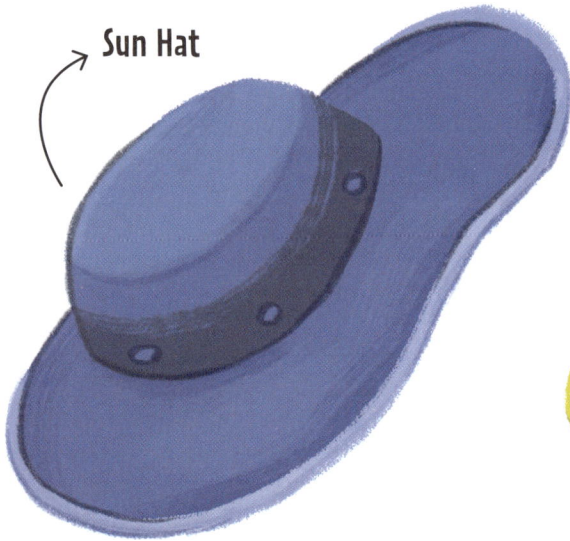

Binoculars

Walking Stick

Picnic Blanket

Picnic Basket